States of Matter

Solids

by Rebecca Pettiford

Bullfrog Books

Ideas for Parents and Teachers

Bullfrog Books let children practice reading informational text at the earliest reading levels. Repetition, familiar words, and photo labels support early readers.

Before Reading
- Discuss the cover photo. What does it tell them?
- Look at the picture glossary together. Read and discuss the words.

During Reading
- "Walk" through the book with the reader. Discuss new or unfamiliar words. Sound them out together.
- Look at the photos together. Point out the photo labels.

After Reading
- Prompt the child to think more. Ask: Look around. What objects are solids? How do you know?

Bullfrog Books are published by Jump!
5357 Penn Avenue South
Minneapolis, MN 55419
www.jumplibrary.com

Copyright © 2026 Jump! International copyright reserved in all countries. No part of this book may be reproduced in any form without written permission from the publisher.

Jump! is a division of FlutterBee Education Group.

Library of Congress Cataloging-in-Publication Data is available at www.loc.gov or upon request from the publisher.

ISBN: 979-8-89213-969-4 (hardcover)
ISBN: 979-8-89213-970-0 (paperback)
ISBN: 979-8-89213-971-7 (ebook)

Editor: Jenna Gleisner
Designer: Anna Peterson

Photo Credits: Vladimir Prusakov/Shutterstock, cover; Jiri Hera/Shutterstock, 1; TaniaKitura/Shutterstock, 3; Oleg Troino/Dreamstime, 4; Andrey Danilovich/iStock, 5, 23br; Jure Divich/Shutterstock, 6–7, 23tr; Kosolovskyy/iStock, 8–9 (foreground); Pixel-Shot/Shutterstock, 8–9 (background); T.Photo/Shutterstock, 10–11; Anatoliy Karlyuk/Shutterstock, 12 (hand); bogdan ionescu/Shutterstock, 12 (sand); Megan Betteridge/Shutterstock, 13 (man); Shestakov Dmytro/Shutterstock, 13 (rock); Luis Molinero/Shutterstock, 14–15; xamtiw/iStock, 16, 23bl; 19 STUDIO/Shutterstock, 17; Bill Sykes/Getty, 18–19, 23tm; Deepak Sethi/iStock, 20–21, 23tl; erierika/iStock, 22 (left); timquo/Shutterstock, 22 (right); Nai_Pisage/Shutterstock, 24.

Printed in the United States of America at Corporate Graphics in North Mankato, Minnesota.

Table of Contents

Hard Shapes	4
Make Ice Pops	22
Picture Glossary	23
Index	24
To Learn More	24

Hard Shapes

We skate on ice.

Ice is hard.
It is a **solid**.

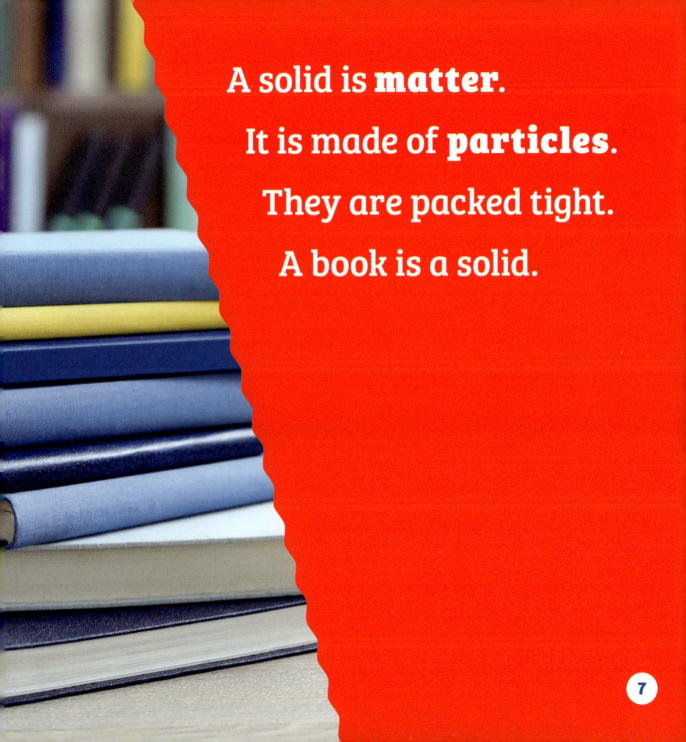

A solid is **matter**.
It is made of **particles**.
They are packed tight.
A book is a solid.

Solids have shapes.
We can hold them.
A pencil is a solid.

Solids take up space.
Ann collects coins.
They fill up a jar.

Solids come in all sizes.
A grain of sand is small.

grain of sand

Gus climbs a rock.

It is big!

Solids can be hard or soft.

A pillow is a solid.

It is soft.

Some solids change.
Ice **melts**.

Now it is water!

Water is a **liquid**.

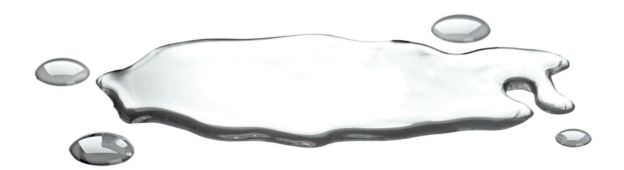

juice

Juice is, too.

Can it be a solid?

Yes!

It **freezes**.

It makes ice pops.

Yum!

Make Ice Pops

Let's freeze liquid juice into yummy, solid treats! Ask an adult for help.

What You Need:
- ice pop molds
- fruit juice

Steps:
1. Pour juice into the molds. Leave a small space at the top.
2. Put on the lids.
3. Place the molds in the freezer.
4. Freeze overnight until they are solid.
5. Enjoy!

Picture Glossary

freezes
Becomes solid or turns into ice at a very low temperature.

liquid
A substance that flows and can be poured.

matter
Something that has weight and takes up space, such as a solid, liquid, or gas.

melts
Changes from a solid to a liquid.

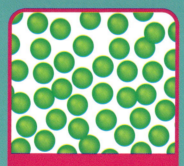

particles
Extremely small pieces of something.

solid
A three-dimensional object.

Index

hard 5, 15
ice 4, 5, 16, 20
juice 19
liquid 17
matter 7
melts 16
particles 7
shapes 8
sizes 12
soft 15
space 11
water 17

To Learn More

Finding more information is as easy as 1, 2, 3.

❶ Go to **www.factsurfer.com**

❷ Enter "**solids**" into the search box.

❸ Choose your book to see a list of websites.

24